WE HEART

50

REASONS

YOUR DREAM

BOYFRIEND

HARRY

STYLES

IS

PERFECTION

HARRY

Harry was only 16 when he auditioned for The X Factor, singing Stevie Wonder's "ISN'T SHE LOVELY" a capella.

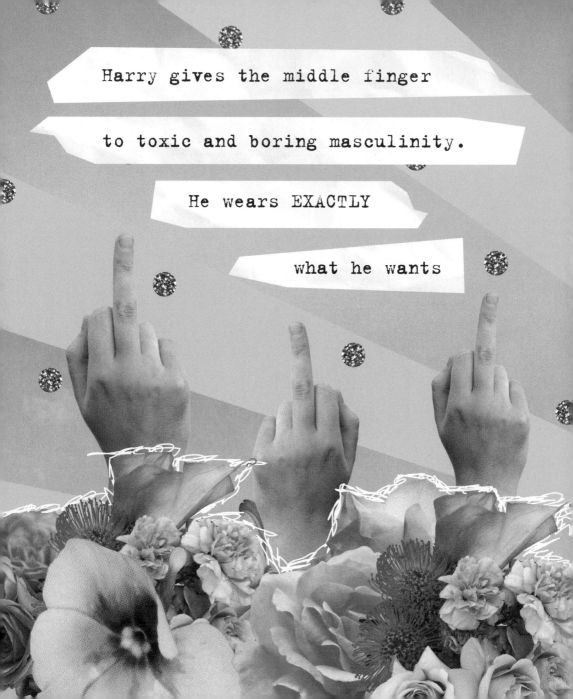

Harry gives the middle finger

to toxic and boring masculinity.

He wears EXACTLY

what he wants

AND LOOKS...

FABULOUSSS.

As an after-school job, Harry slung pastries at W. Mandeville Bakery.

His former boss said that "He was the most polite member of staff we've ever had."

IS ANYONE EVEN SURPRISED?

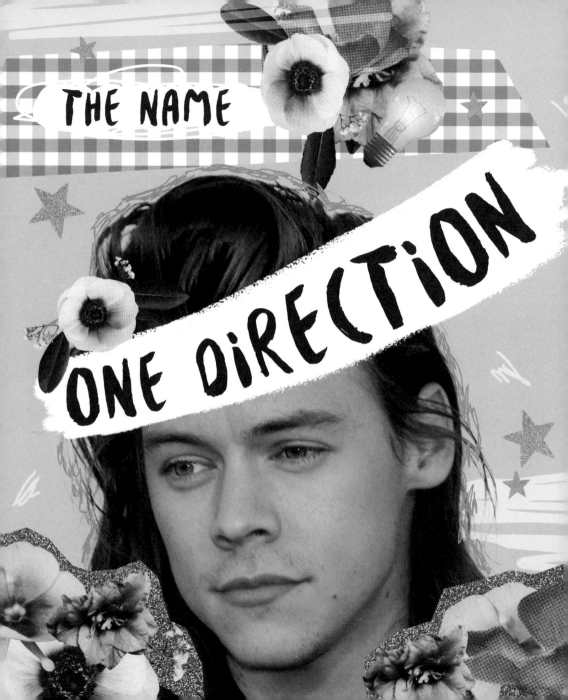

THE NAME

ONE DiRECTION

WAS HARRY'S IDEA.

With those two words,
he changed the direction
of pop music history

FOREVER.

Harry is unabashedly schmaltzy.

He loves romcoms and his favorite films are tear-jerkers – The Notebook, Love Actually, and Titanic.

PASS THE TISSUES,

PLEASE.

He's an

AQUARIUS.

As a fellow air sign,
that makes us a perfect

COSMIC MATCH.

(JUST SAYIN...)

One Direction never won
The X Factor.

Instead,

they came third

and proceeded to casually take over

THE WORLD,

becoming one of the best-selling

boy bands

OF ALL TIME.

Growing up, Harry had a pet hamster.

In a sign of
the creativity
that would
make him   into a

MEGASTAR,

HARRY NAMED iT...   HAMSTER.

His fisrt celebrity crush was

JENNiFER ANiSTON.

I would ship
that couple.

WHEN HARRY WAS

15,

he spent nearly all his after-school wages on long train trips to visit his first girlfriend.

Harry stands up for his
legions of superfans:

"How can you say young
girls don't get it?

They're our future.

Our future doctors,

lawyers,

mothers,

presidents.

They kind of keep the world going."

Harry is **COVERED** in tattoos, including an anatomical human heart on his left bicep.

He literally wears his heart

on his sleeve.

as a cheeky

protest until the owner of

@harrystyles finally

handed over the reins.

Harry and Lizzo are OBSESSED with each other.

Nothing is more **iCONiC** than the footage of "Hizzo" flirting and giggling over

TEQUiLA

at the 2020 Brit Awards.

He made his

acting debut in

CHRISTOPHER

NOLAN'S

adrenaline-fueled

DUNKiRK,

looking damn **FiNE**

in a uniform.

HARRY'S PARTIAL TO VINTAGE CARS.

He can take us for a ride around London in his primrose yellow '73 Jaguar

ANY TIME.

TELEPHONE

PULL

HE KNOWS HOW TO PARTY.

Harry bought a new mattress to celebrate "Up All Night" topping the US charts.

Harry paid tribute to

CLUELESS

character Cher Horowitz on the 2021 Grammy's red carpet in full Gucci.

From the plaid blazer to the
purple feather boa, this look
had the internet, like,

TOTALLY

BUGGiN!

Grammy? Yep. Brit Award? Sure.
People's Choice Awards? Obvi.

Harry's surely tracking for

EGOT STATUS.

HARRY IS A GENEROUS

KING!

Aside from his formal philanthropy, he used a day off in LA to buy and hand deliver $3000 worth of pizza to the homeless.

ACCORDING

TO HIS SISTER,

Harry used to wear a

hand-me-down dalmatian outfit

an INORDINATE amount

of the time'.

Despite being one of

the **BiGGEST**

pop stars on the planet,

Harry used to get

major stage fright.

And somehow that makes

him even CUTER.

His precious mum, Anne, was the one who submitted his *X-Factor* application.

CHEERS, MUM!

Harry really puts the

STYLE iN HARRY STYLES.

He's risen to GOD-TIER status in the fashion world,

co-chairing the Met Gala in 2019 and becoming the first man to appear solo on a *Vogue* cover.

STEVIE NICKS

has been Harry's close friend since they met backstage at a

FLEETWOOD MAC CONCERT in 2015.

It was Stevie's birthday, and Harry appeared with a cake complete with her name hand-piped on top.

Harry says that his

FRIENDSHIPS

are the most

valuable thing

in his life.

CRYING EMOJI

Once, Harry's car broke down in front of a fan's house. She wasn't home (can you imagine???), but her dad let Harry in to use the phone.

Harry left her an
adorable note and
even fed her fish.

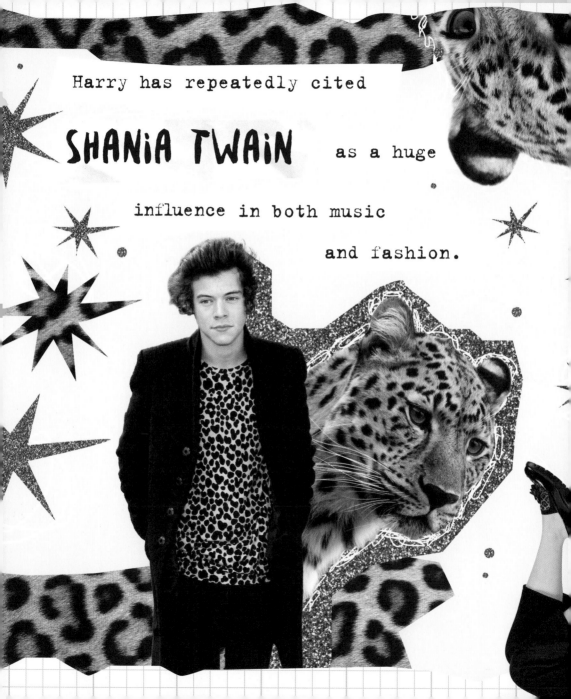

Harry has repeatedly cited

SHANiA TWAiN

as a huge

influence in both music

and fashion.

You might say that she

DOES, INDEED,

impress him much.

HE'S FUNNY.

Never was this more
evident than when Harry hosted

THE LATE LATE SHOW

the day James Cordon's
daughter was born.

Harry has spoken openly
and honestly about his mental health,
encouraging others to try
therapy and engage in mindfulness.

#Be kind

Harry grew up with a

KARAOKE MACHINE.

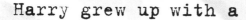

He'd entertain his
grandparents with
Elvis renditions, but
his favorite track
was always

"ENDLESS LOVE"

by Diana Ross and Lionel Richie.

"Watermelon Sugar" got the internet feelin'

HOT
AND
HEAVY,

with thirsty fans deciding

THE SONG'S LYRICS CELEBRATE

A CERTAIN

type of lovemaking.

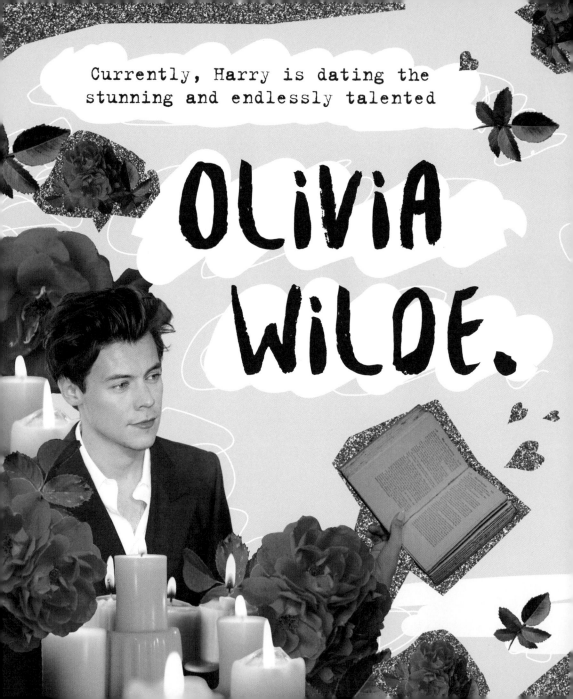

Currently, Harry is dating the stunning and endlessly talented

OLiViA WiLDE.

Together they are the
power couple to end all
power couples.

Harry's ever-

BLOSSOMING

solo career has defied

the trajectory

of most boy band alumni.

We stan a

well-mannered,

ENGLISH

GENTLEMAN.

Harry is famously punctual

and polite to

everyone he meets.

FOR ANYONE

who wants
to claim

he doesn't
have talent,

Harry can also juggle
and play the

KAZOO.

iN HiS ONE DiRECTiON DAYS,

the band recorded their albums on the road, in a van with no air conditioning.

Harry has worked

(and sweated)

for his fame.

Once, Harry managed to get a rare picture beside a smiling Van Morrison.

Harry jokes that he got Van to crack a grin by tickling him on the back.

OH, TO BE THAT BACK.

On the set of the

"WATERMEL

ON SUGAR"

music video, Harry set a clear
standard of consent for physical contact
between the cast.

WE LOVE TO SEE iT!

Harry had to **CHOP OFF HIS** luxurious One Direction **LOCKS** to film Dunkirk.

He donated his hair to a British charity that makes wigs for kids undergoing cancer treatment.

The intense online fandom surrounding Harry inspired the critically acclaimed (and stupidly funny) Australian musical Fangirls.

IT'S A MUST SEE/LISTEN FOR HARRY STANS.

HE LOOOOVES APPLE JUICE.

SO. DAMN.

WHOLESOME.

Harry's second solo album

FINE LINE

was included in Rolling Stone's
"500 Greatest Albums

OF

ALL

TIME"

in 2020.

How many former boy band members can claim that?

His list of song
writing credits
includes tracks for

ARIANA
GRANDE,

MEGHAN
TRAINOR

AND
MICHEAL
BUBLÉ.

He's also collaborated with

TAYLOR SWIFT,

JOHN LEGEND,

AND BRUNO MARS.

HE CALLS HiS MUM
UP TO FiVE TiMES

A DAY!

Harry says a school play might have kicked off his flair for fashion.

He played a church mouse named Barney and the costume included his first-ever pair of tights.

I'm sure the performance was moving.

The following statement is presented without comment:

the first gig

Harry ever attended

was a

NiCKELBACK

concert in Manchester.

Harry donated

a whopping

$1.2 M

iLLiON

to charity after

his first solo tour.

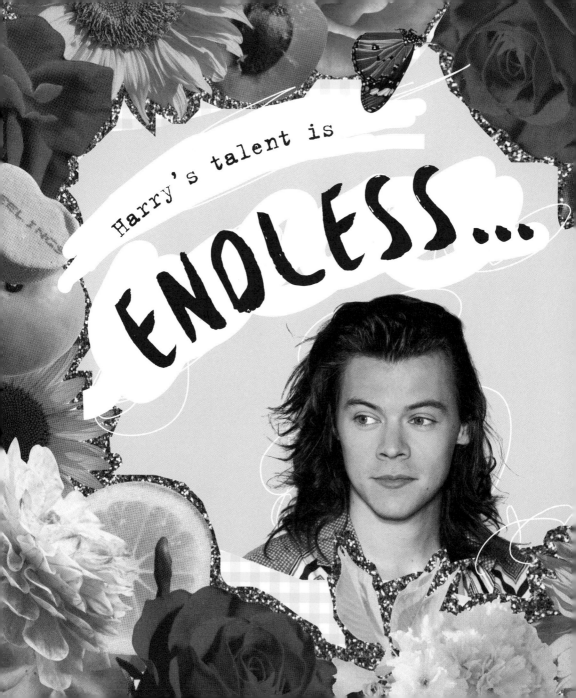

Harry's talent is

ENDLESS...